ARIES

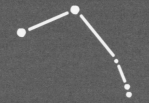

A GUIDED JOURNAL

Constance Stellas

ADAMS MEDIA
New York London Toronto Sydney New Delhi

Adams Media
An Imprint of Simon & Schuster, Inc.
100 Technology Center Drive
Stoughton, Massachusetts 02072

First Adams Media hardcover edition September 2022

ADAMS MEDIA and colophon are trademarks of Simon & Schuster.

For information about special discounts for bulk purchases, please contact Simon & Schuster Special Sales at 1-866-506-1949 or business@simonandschuster.com.

The Simon & Schuster Speakers Bureau can bring authors to your live event. For more information or to book an event contact the Simon & Schuster Speakers Bureau at 1-866-248-3049 or visit our website at www.simonspeakers.com.

Interior design by Colleen Cunningham
Interior illustrations by Tess Armstrong
Interior images © Getty Images/Vikiss, Mara Fribus; Simon & Schuster, Inc.

Manufactured in China

10 9 8 7 6 5 4 3 2 1

ISBN 978-1-5072-1948-5

CONTENTS

INTRODUCTION

Are you interested in how the stars may influence your characteristics? Wanting a little celestial insight into how you can strengthen your relationships? Looking for guidance in using your energetic, forceful talents? Guided journaling can be a dialogue between your thoughts, feelings, and aspects of your sign and element. By reflecting in an intentional way, you can begin to understand yourself—and how you interact with the world around you—better.

A fire sign, Aries is an impetuous, fervent pioneer. The sheer verve and energy of this first sign can accomplish many things if you complete one project before starting another. Journaling can help you keep track of all your great plans so you can tackle them one by one. Have you noticed that your relationships begin with great expectations and passion, but many times the ardor wanes and you move on? The prompts in this book will allow you to explore all the social parts of your personality and help you consider sticking with a relationship that has potential by exploring your Aries tendencies and what you may share with other fire signs.

Journaling can also help Aries explore ways to cool his hot temper. Your symbol, the ram, sometimes butts his head against difficulties and challenges—usually in service of personal or societal justice (which is a good way of expressing your energy!). However, when unchecked, Aries becomes a hothead, fighting everything and everyone. After all, your ruler is Mars, the god of war, and your battles are worthy and important. But can you remember a time when you fought for a principle and were not successful because of the way you went about fighting for it? By reflecting on the prompts in this book, you will gain a deeper understanding of how you can make your valiant efforts successful.

When you write, you connect with your feelings, desires, and everything in between. And when prompts drive you to contemplate the wealth of astrological wisdom that each element and Sun sign offers, it can lead to surprising, creative insights. Maybe you knew that you have abundant, joyful energy but didn't realize that this joy can enthuse, lead, and inspire others. Or perhaps you had never considered that you need to relax from time to time—after all, you are at risk for burnout because of your high energy levels. This book will help you explore yourself and your place among the stars.

HOW TO USE THIS BOOK

Welcome to your astrology journal! This guided journal is divided into three parts to help you explore your connections to the stars.

PART ONE

First, there are prompts about astrology in general, from how you feel about astrological wisdom to what you notice about your relationships with different signs and your experiences with reading horoscopes. The long and rich history of astrology can truly enhance your life and deepen your self-knowledge. Whatever strikes your fancy is a prompt to pursue! The purpose is not to master celestial knowledge but to turn your thoughts to the cosmos and reflect in an intentional way that may uncover some surprising insights.

PART TWO

The second part features prompts about your element. In astrology, there are four elements:

- Fire
- Earth
- Air
- Water

There are three zodiac signs in each element.

THE
PASSIONATE
FIRE SIGNS
ARE:

 ARIES

 LEO

 SAGITTARIUS

THE
PRACTICAL
EARTH SIGNS
ARE:

 TAURUS

 VIRGO

 CAPRICORN

THE
COMMUNICATIVE
AIR SIGNS
ARE:

 GEMINI

 LIBRA

 AQUARIUS

THE
EMOTIONAL
WATER SIGNS
ARE:

 CANCER

 SCORPIO

PISCES

All members of the same element have an affinity; being with your elemental brothers or sisters can often feel comfortable because they speak your language. Understanding the characteristics of your element can give insight into good health practices and ways to relax and recharge, as well as how you might approach aspects of life such as work and relationships.

PART THREE

Finally, the third part of this journal concentrates on your Sun sign. This is the position of the sun when you were born. The Sun sign is a dominant feature in a person's entire chart. It reveals your:

- Psychological characteristics
- Health habits
- Relationship affinities
- Spiritual mission in this lifetime

Each Sun sign also has a ruling planet that gives the sign a certain kind of energy; a symbol that represents the characteristics of the sign's personality; and a modality that reveals whether that sign charges ahead in life, prefers the security of things remaining the same, or is open to the changes that come along. Consider these prompts intuitively. When something speaks to you and you think "Yes! That's me," reflect on the questions and any suggestions posed by the prompt. If you don't feel particularly drawn to a prompt, you may want to return to it later. If the information or questions in a prompt make you feel uncomfortable, consider whether there is something hidden or suppressed in your life that it awakens. Or you may use the page to explore why this doesn't fit you. True, not every aspect of the Sun sign will resonate with every person, so you may want to look at your full birth chart to help color the portrait of you that you create in this journal.

Astrology has become more and more popular, thanks to the ease of calculating birth charts online; the availability of daily, weekly, or monthly horoscopes delivered straight to your inbox; popular lists of famous people according to their Sun signs; and more. Ancient astrologers may have appreciated these options, *but* a computer is not a person, and the information that computer printouts offer is standard. Anyone born on the same day, time, year, and place as you would have the same astrology chart; however, people are individuals. There's a lot more to you than what is written about a Sun sign or astrological element. The beauty of this journal is that you can reflect on what astrology means to *you* and understand the nuances of your sign and element and how they do or don't relate to you as a unique person. Use this journal as your guide in exploring what the stars can teach you about yourself!

Astrology is the study of star and planetary patterns and what they mean for individuals and societies. Observing the regular motions of the sun, the moon, and other planets, ancient people became adept at interpreting what these celestial bodies and cycles meant. Today, there is a new renaissance in astrology, thanks to the Internet. Now anyone can find out the locations of the sun, the moon, Venus, and more at the time of their birth in just seconds, and subscribe to a service featuring daily, weekly, and monthly astrological forecasts. Consulting astrologers also offer star wisdom for health, business dealings, romance, spiritual development, and marriage.

In this part, you'll find thought-provoking prompts to guide you in reflecting on astrology in a more general context, rather than focusing on one specific sign or element. The sun, the moon, Mercury, Venus, Mars, Jupiter, Saturn, Uranus, Neptune, and Pluto: All of these celestial energies make up a natal chart and become a blueprint for gaining deeper self-knowledge and guiding your life. You can explore the astrological patterns in your family, track how different events like eclipses and equinoxes impact your mood and experiences, consider your beliefs on fate versus free will, and more. Enjoy this journey into the cosmos.

PART ONE
GETTING TO KNOW THE WORLD OF ASTROLOGY

Imagine you are lying on the grass or a beach or sitting on a bench at night. You can see the stars, perhaps the moon. Depending on the time of year, you might even see Venus twinkling on the horizon or a distant red glow from Mars. Describe what you feel. Awe? Like you are part of the universe? Or like you are insignificant compared to the vast celestial sky? Maybe curious to know more about the heavens?

If you were an ancient navigator and only had the constellations and the moon with which to navigate your ship to get home, would you feel comforted by the regularity of the patterns in the night sky? Write about a time when you felt lost literally or emotionally. Did the moon or a twinkling star give you courage? Did you notice if the moon during that time was just a crescent or full? Or maybe it was somewhere in between?

Astrology has become more and more popular in recent years, thanks to the Internet! Do you believe that everything astrology says about your sign is true? Write about a positive experience you have had reading your horoscope. Did you follow the advice? What happened?

What charms you about astrology? What bothers or concerns you about it? Are you mindful of the monthly zodiac sign changes? Describe any feelings you have about how certain zodiac time periods affect you. For example, in spring, when the sun is in Aries, maybe you feel energized.

Are there certain signs with which you are more harmonious? Less harmonious? Write about your experiences.

....
....
....
....
....
....
....
....
....
....
....
....
....
....
....
....
....
....
....
....
....
....
....
....
....
....

A person's fate or destiny is a lifelong path. Describe how you feel when you read an astrological prediction for your future. Do you think it is good to know this information? Or better not to know? Do you use this information, keep it in mind, or ignore it?

....
....
....
....
....
....
....
....
....
....
....
....
....
....
....
....
....
....
....
....
....
....
....
....
....
....

Each zodiac sign is ruled by a planet or by the Sun or the Moon. Do you identify with Mercury, Venus, Mars, Jupiter, Saturn, Uranus, Neptune, Pluto, the Sun, or the Moon? Is it the planet your sign is ruled by? If not, describe your feelings about your own sign's planet. Do you think knowing more about your planet brings you insights into your personality or fortune?

....
....
....
....
....
....
....
....
....
....
....
....
....
....
....
....
....
....
....
....
....
....
....
....

....
....
....
....
....
....
....
....
....
....
....
....
....
....
....
....
....
....
....
....
....
....
....
....
....
....
....
....
....
....
....
....
....

The most famous—or infamous!—astrological event is Mercury Retrograde. This happens three times each year and means that Mercury appears to be moving backward in relation to the earth's orbit. It is common during these periods to experience electronic mishaps, communications going awry, and difficulties and delays in scheduling. Describe any Mercury Retrograde experiences you may have noticed. Were you forced to be more patient than usual?

If your Sun is in Gemini or Virgo, both signs ruled by Mercury, you may experience more personal confusion during Mercury in retrograde. Describe any personal confusion that you or your Gemini or Virgo friends experience at this time. Did you notice that you or they felt relief when Mercury was no longer retrograde?

....
....
....
....
....
....
....
....
....
....
....
....
....
....
....
....
....
....
....
....
....
....
....
....
....

The moon is our closest celestial neighbor, and its rhythms influence daily life. The monthly new moon marks the beginning of the moon's phases. At the new moon, people make wishes or set intentions with support from the moon's increasing energy as she waxes toward the full moon (the peak of lunar energy). Do you tend to notice the moon's phase, influence, or sign? Write about your relationship with and feeling toward this light.

Many astrologers believe that a person's chart can indicate past lives. What historical time period do you feel connected to? Who do you feel you might have been in a past life? What was your profession? Do you believe a past life can influence your present life? If so, how?

....
....
....
....
....
....
....
....
....
....
....
....
....
....
....
....
....
....
....
....
....
....
....
....

Each astrological sign is either masculine or feminine. This designation has nothing to do with gender or sexual orientation. The masculine signs radiate outwardly, and the feminine signs inwardly. Make a list of all the signs in your birth chart. Which energy dominates? Or perhaps they are equal? Do you feel these descriptions are true to your self-image?

In astrology, each sign has a symbol associated with it. Think about the symbol for your sign. Explore your feelings toward this symbol. Do any of its characteristics apply to you? You might write a story about yourself and what your symbol means to you. For example, as a Leo, are you more like a roaring lion or a purring cat?

As you will discover in this guided journey, there are four elements: fire, earth, air, and water. Each sign belongs to one element. Have you noticed that the signs of people you get along with have the same element as you do? Or a certain different element? Write about your experiences with people of the same and different elements.

....
....
....
....
....
....
....
....
....
....
....
....
....
....
....
....
....
....
....
....
....
....
....

Some people believe that following astrology curtails free will by forecasting the future. Do you believe this? Do you think it is possible that by knowing about your sign and using the stars as guides for the future you can make better choices in your life? Or do you feel controlled by what the stars say? Reflect on your feelings about free will and the stars.

....

....

....

....

....

....

....

....

....

....

....

....

....

....

....

....

....

....

....

....

....

....

....

Throughout the history of astrology, healers and physicians were required to study the positions of the planets in order to help their patients. They believed that the planetary energies could help or hinder healing the soul and body. What do you think about this idea? Can you implement any of your astrological insights into your health practices?

....
....
....
....
....
....
....
....
....
....
....
....
....
....
....
....
....
....
....
....
....
....

The position of the sun, the moon, and the ascendant are the three most important placements in a person's natal chart. If you know your birth time, you can easily determine these with the help of an app or astrology website. Explore your astrological trio and write down your feelings about these placements. Do you feel more connected to your moon or to your ascendant? Are there any patterns you notice, like the same element for each placement?

....
....
....
....
....
....
....
....
....
....
....
....
....
....
....
....
....
....
....
....
....
....
....

Eclipses were awesome phenomena for the ancients—and still have us in awe today! In a total solar eclipse, the sun's light is blocked by the moon, and the atmosphere darkens. In a lunar eclipse, the moon is blocked by the earth, and we cannot see this silvery orb. Most years have four eclipses. Do you pay attention to this heavenly event? Do you notice any patterns, either within yourself or in your surroundings during an eclipse? Research when the next eclipse will be, and record your feelings for the week leading up to the event.

How do you typically "use" astrology? Do you find it useful for self-understanding? Understanding other people? Exploring your friendships and/or partnerships? Do daily horoscopes guide your actions? Or do you see astrology as more of a guide for larger focuses in life? Write about an experience when an astrological tip helped you in some way.

Have you noticed that people in the same family often have the same signs? Or that other positions in their charts correspond? It's frequently the case! Take a look at your family's and extended family's signs, and reflect on the similarities and differences.

....
....
....
....
....
....
....
....
....
....
....
....
....
....
....
....
....
....
....
....
....
....
....
....
....
....

Saturn is the farthest planet you can see with the naked eye. It rules time, structure, and lessons of life. A major astrological transit is the Saturn Return, when Saturn returns to its natal chart position. This happens between ages twenty-eight and thirty. Where is Saturn in your chart? Have you experienced this return? Whether you have experienced your Saturn Return or not, write about your feelings toward the current path of your life, relationships, health, and spiritual development. If you have experienced your Saturn Return, how did your life look during these years?

Aside from your Saturn Return, another important transit (when a planet returns to its original position in your birth chart) is with the planet Jupiter. Jupiter is called the benefic of the zodiac. He helps us feel generous toward ourselves and others, is good for business, and can bring new areas of creativity into life. Jupiter returns to his birthplace every twelve years. Think about your birthday years at each twelfth year so far. Write about your feelings and activities in those years. Were the experiences positive? Expansive? Creative?

The solstices, summer and winter, occur at opposite signs: Cancer in the summer, and Capricorn in the winter. They mark the height of sunlight in summer and the depths of darkness in winter. How is your mood at these times? Describe how these essential astrological markers affect you.

Two major points in nature and the celestial calendar are the equinoxes: the fall equinox (Libra) and the spring equinox (Aries). These events mean there is equal daylight and darkness during that day. Do you have any particular feelings during these times of the year? Happy fall is coming after a hot summer? Or anticipating spring after a harsh winter? Write your feelings about the rhythm of nature and how it corresponds to your experience of the seasons. If you live in the southern hemisphere, the equinoxes are reversed.

....
....
....
....
....
....
....
....
....
....
....
....
....
....
....
....
....
....
....
....
....
....

If someone you know says, "I don't believe in astrology, it's rubbish," what do you say back? Write a dialogue between you and a skeptical person. What are your points of agreement? Of disagreement?

Have you ever noticed that some days feel lucky and positive and that during other days nothing seems to go right? It could be that the planetary pattern in the sky is not in harmony with your personal planets! Keep a record of good and bad days and the placements of the planets during each day. Reflect on any patterns. (You can find the daily position of the planets online.)

....

....

....

....

....

....

....

....

....

....

....

....

....

....

....

....

....

....

....

....

....

....

....

Throughout history, people have sought to understand the world around them. Today we have scientific equipment to inform us of the makeup of the universe, but ancient peoples could only observe the basic elements that they saw in their lives: fire, earth, air, and water. They associated each of these elements with an astrological sign and certain characteristics, and physicians used these characteristics to treat and heal their patients. The elements and their characteristics are:

FIRE (Aries, Leo, Sagittarius): Fire signs are known for their passionate energy and impetuosity. They often need to moderate their bursts of enthusiasm to prevent burnout.

EARTH (Taurus, Virgo, Capricorn): Earth signs are practical, cautious, and seek out security with a measured pace. Cultivating change and taking a few risks can enhance their lives, boost their health, and encourage flexibility.

AIR (Gemini, Libra, Aquarius): Air signs are changeable and mentally oriented; they enjoy living in creative possibilities and have highly sensitive nervous systems. Getting "down to earth" can help air signs move forward realistically.

WATER (Cancer, Scorpio, Pisces): Water is the element of feelings, and all water signs react to life emotionally. Calming their waves of emotion in order to see a situation clearly is a lifelong challenge for all water signs.

The more than two dozen prompts in this part of the book will give you a platform for understanding more about yourself and your nature based on your element.

PART TWO

GETTING TO KNOW YOUR ELEMENT

In astrology, fire is the first element of creation. Fire provides the spark that ignites passion and brings people together. Fire was also the foundation of communities: It invited people to gather for warmth and protection and to cook food. If you were a primitive human and discovered the warming power of fire, how would you feel? Now think about the current day and describe your favorite experiences with fire, such as campfires, candles, and so on.

One characteristic of all fire signs is their bursts of energy. Once you start, it is difficult to moderate your enthusiasm. Yet without a few rest stops, it can also be easy to burn out. Describe a time when you pushed your energy to the point of exhaustion. What clued you in that you were "running on empty"? How did you recharge your energy?

....

....

....

....

....

....

....

....

....

....

....

....

....

....

....

....

....

....

....

....

....

....

Mars, the Sun, and Jupiter are the planets that rule fire signs; each is a ball of energy and power. Mars symbolizes warlike fire; the Sun, health-giving exuberance; and Jupiter, spiritual and physical expansion. Do you feel compatible energies when you speak or interact with fellow fire signs (Aries, Leo, and Sagittarius)? Write down the adjectives that you feel describe your "clan."

In Greek mythology, Prometheus gave fire to mortals because he had such affection for people on Earth. He was punished for this deed, but civilization grew from his gift. What do you consider the greatest blessing of fire for humans? Write down your feelings about this essential element.

Fire can be beautiful, but it can also burn and destroy. Many weapons get their power from fire in one form or another. Write down your feelings about destructive firepower. How could this manifest itself in your life?

....
....
....
....
....
....
....
....
....
....
....
....
....
....
....
....
....
....
....
....
....
....
....

Fire signs are temperamental because their energy insists on burning freely. Describe a time when your anger was stoked and yielded positive results. Conversely, write about a time when you contained the blaze and benefited from moderation.

At the beginning of recorded history, fire brought hunters into communities and encouraged agriculture. Slowly, fire was used to cook food. Today, many fire signs become expert chefs. Think about whether or not you like to cook. What are your favorite tastes and recipes? Describe any important experiences you have had cooking for yourself and/or others.

Today, fire glows in fireplaces or decorates our homes in the form of candles. What is your favorite way to appreciate fire? Describe a personal experience with the glow of embers, a barbecue, or a candlelit room.

Enthusiasm is the lifeblood of all fire signs. Even if it seems like nothing is going on in your life, you will find something to be enthusiastic about. In fact, fire signs sometimes play a game with themselves and make the most ordinary chores dramatic, exciting, and interesting. Describe a time when you encouraged yourself by making a game of a tedious task.

Fire is the element of spirit and is used in rituals to purify and cleanse. Describe any purifying experiences or feelings you have had with fire. What did you do, and what were the results?

The element fire is fundamentally a creative force, and fire signs can use their fire power in unsuspecting ways. Fire people often have "hunches" about opportunities or relationships. When their powerful energy is kindled, they find lucky opportunities or connect with people who can help them. Write about any lucky hunches that led you to a positive conclusion.

Health is usually robust among fire signs. Describe your own health routine. If you do not feel robust and suffer from low energy, examine your emotional life and see if something is creating a firewall that is smothering your natural exuberance.

....
....
....
....
....
....
....
....
....
....
....
....
....
....
....
....
....
....
....
....
....
....
....
....

In relationships, marriage, or dating, fire people want adventure and experiences. Nice dinners with candlelight are fine, but a special experience with perhaps a bit of danger is really the way to keep your love life's fires burning. Write about the best adventure you and a fire partner had. How did it move your relationship forward?

....
....
....
....
....
....
....
....
....
....
....
....
....
....
....
....
....
....
....
....
....
....
....
....

Which element do you imagine is most compatible with fire signs? (Here's a clue: Fire needs air to burn.) Describe how you connect with air signs, then write about relationships you have with each of the other elements: water, fire, and earth.

Which element is opposite to the fire signs? (Here's a clue: Water puts fire out.) Write about a positive or negative connection or relationship with any of the water signs: Cancer, Scorpio, or Pisces.

....
....
....
....
....
....
....
....
....
....
....
....
....
....
....
....
....
....
....
....
....
....
....
....
....
....
....

....
....
....
....
....
....
....
....
....
....
....
....
....
....
....
....
....
....
....
....
....
....
....
....
....
....
....
....
....

In the general pace of life, fire signs move quickly. Do you walk quickly? Does it annoy you to be slowed down by people ambling along? If you are in a car, do you drive fast? Have you received speeding tickets? Describe your ideal pace.

Which astrological element do you think would make an ideal world leader: fire, earth, air, or water? Why? Describe your ideal leader.

A fever is the body's way of burning up illness and infection. Most fire signs run a higher temperature than normal, and their fevers can be higher than for other elements. Have you experienced this? What are your best remedies for fevers? Describe your experiences with fevers.

....
....
....
....
....
....
....
....
....
....
....
....
....
....
....
....
....
....
....
....
....
....
....
....

Enthusiastic spontaneity is a common impulse for all fire signs. In what ways is this part of your character? Write about the last time when, on impulse, you decided to do something fun. Were you alone or with a partner/friend? Describe your feelings about this adventure.

Intimacy and sex are prime ways that fire signs show their passion. They love to feel close and share their passions, and flirting is a good way to start. Describe a time when flirting led to a closer relationship. Then write down what you imagine an ideal passionate relationship would look and feel like.

A single flame is a particularly good image to focus on during meditation. The blue center or the yellow/red aura glowing outwardly can calm your feelings as you breathe deeply. In times of stress, see if meditating on a single candle flame can help you calm down and focus. Write about your experiences.

Red is the primary color associated with fire. It symbolizes bravery, courage, anger, and passion. Write down how you feel about the color red. Does it suit you to wear red clothes? If you imagine the color red, what do you feel?

Some alternative healers associate different sounds with elements. Laughter is the sound connected to the fire element. Describe the best joke you ever heard. Does it still make you laugh? Write about the qualities of your laughter and your loved ones' laughter.

Fire signs are creative. This guided journal is just one way to spark your creativity—jot down some other ways here. Write the ideas down without judgment; you don't need to act on each one. After a few days, review your list and decide which ideas to bring to fruition, then describe your experiences.

A nature hike is the best exercise for fire signs. You will feel free,
move your limbs, and take in the amazing views. Write about the
best experience you have had with nature hikes. How did you feel
afterward?

....

....

....

....

....

....

....

....

....

....

....

....

....

....

....

....

....

....

....

....

....

....

....

....

....

Have you ever considered burning up the papers, letters, or written "evidence" that you keep from a worn-out relationship? Destruction by fire is final and can free up your energy for new experiences. Write about a time when you safely burned the record of a difficult relationship or situation. How did you feel afterward?

....

....

....

....

....

....

....

....

....

....

....

....

....

....

....

....

....

....

....

....

....

....

....

The twelve astrological signs we know today come from the twelve constellations arranged around the ecliptic of the sun's path. Astrologers observe these signs and interpret their effect on people and events. For example, an astrologer may note that as a Virgo, a person might be great at analysis but find it challenging to synthesize all the details. And a Scorpio may be drawn to jobs or a certain career where they can investigate people or subjects, but a corporate structure doesn't appeal to them. Through understanding your Sun sign, you have a unique window of insight into yourself and your life!

The prompts in this part will guide you through a deeper exploration of your Sun sign and the traits, relationship dynamics, and more that may be influenced by this sign. Reflect on how your career path may be impacted by your sign. Consider how a certain characteristic linked to your sign plays into how you handle conflict with friends. Through guided journaling, this part will help you get to know yourself better. Of course, there is much more to astrology than your personal Sun sign. If you are interested in knowing even more about your relationship with the cosmos, you can also look at the other signs in your birth chart, such as your ascendant sign. Or you may want to focus more deeply on general astrology, as well as your Sun sign and sign element, and revisit different prompts to see how your reflections may evolve. This is *your* astrological journey: Let it take you wherever you want to go!

PART THREE
GETTING TO KNOW YOUR SIGN

Aries is a pioneer who isn't afraid to take the first step to start things off. But astrologers say Aries is sometimes like champagne: lots of bubbles, then flat. In other words, Aries energy is strong when initiating projects, then it wanes if the project isn't going well or another interesting project comes along. Describe a time when you started a business venture or personal project. Were you able to maintain your enthusiasm throughout the process? Write about the beginning, middle, and finish of this endeavor.

Mars, the ruling planet for Aries, is the god of war and signifies physical strength and skill. What is your favorite way to exercise—as a team or in solo pursuit? What new activities do you want to try? Write down your current exercise regimen and any fitness goals you have.

....
....
....
....
....
....
....
....
....
....
....
....
....
....
....
....
....
....
....
....
....
....
....
....
....

Aries may need to discharge some of their powerful energy when they feel frustrated or angry. Describe how you deal with big feelings, whether it's going to kickboxing class, screaming into a pillow, or banging pots and pans. How would you change any of your habits?

....
....
....
....
....
....
....
....
....
....
....
....
....
....
....
....
....
....
....
....
....
....
....
....

Mars is the planet that rules sickness that subsides quickly. Aries (and other fire signs) often run high fevers that seem to burn up illnesses in no time. In what ways do illnesses typically show up in your body? What steps do you take to avoid or minimize everyday sicknesses?

....
....
....
....
....
....
....
....
....
....
....
....
....
....
....
....
....
....
....
....
....
....
....
....
....

Every zodiac sign rules a part of the body—Aries rules the head, sinuses, and brow. Some Aries people sustain injuries to the head or have sinus problems. Do you find yourself prone to head injury or illness? Describe things you notice about your head, sinus, or brow health and how you can protect these areas from harm. (Remember, if you ride a bike or motorcycle, *always* wear a helmet!)

Mars is a planet with a reddish hue that is visible in the sky at various times of the year. Do you feel connected to your ruler? Would you like to be a space pioneer and travel to Mars? Think about planning a Mars viewing night with your Aries friends where you discuss the possibility of visiting your ruling planet. Write your thoughts about the topic here.

Aries is a strong defender of justice and protection for the underdog. Describe a time when you defended a movement or cause. What organizations or causes are you passionate about? What short- and long-term goals do you want to achieve in these causes?

....
....
....
....
....
....
....
....
....
....
....
....
....
....
....
....
....
....
....
....
....
....
....
....
....
....

Some Aries experience burnout because they run at high levels of energy all the time. What do you do to relax and regather your strength? How often do you find yourself exhausted? Do you press on or allow yourself to rest for a while? Describe your awareness of your energy levels and your relaxation choices.

....
....
....
....
....
....
....
....
....
....
....
....
....
....
....
....
....
....
....
....
....
....
....

Red is Aries' color. Wearing black, as many people do nowadays, depresses Aries' energy. Do you like the color red? Describe your feelings about the color and wearing it. Have you had any experiences when wearing red for courage and bravery motivated you?

Aries usually enjoys strong cardio exercise like running to express their physical energy. Sprinters push for bursts of high speed, while long-distance runners opt for a steady pace and measure their energy. If you're a runner, describe your feeling of "the runner's high" and which type of running encourages that for you. If running is not your sport, notice whether you feel a high from exercising in short bursts or via prolonged energy. Describe your preferred pace.

....
....
....
....
....
....
....
....
....
....
....
....
....
....
....
....
....
....
....
....
....
....

Every sign has a purpose in the development and evolution of the human soul. As the first sign and the beginning of spring, Aries' purpose is to ignite the spark of life that begins the soul's journey—much like a child's experience. There is a childlike quality to Aries that is both endearing and enticing. Do you feel that your inner child is thriving? In what ways? Write about how you care for, encourage, and love your inner child.

Aries is usually a risk-taker. Do you take risks, emotionally, professionally, or physically? Describe a time when you were hesitant and then blazed ahead, taking a risk. Write about your feelings before you began and then how the experiences progressed. Did this experience change your feeling about risks in general?

Green, symbolizing spring and all nature burgeoning, is also an Aries color. Malachite is a green stone that energetically boosts Aries. You can wear malachite jewelry or find a raw, uncut stone to carry in a pocket on the left side of your body; this is the receptive side of the body. Write down your feelings and any unusual experiences you have when wearing malachite.

Your symbol, the ram, likes to roam the fields and is able to deal with any climate. Desert heat often suits Aries. Write about which type of climate you prefer.

....
....
....
....
....
....
....
....
....
....
....
....
....
....
....
....
....
....
....
....
....
....
....
....
....
....
....
....

Every sign has a shadow side that describes what the sign needs to master in this lifetime. For Aries, it is managing their temper. Aries' temper tends to flare up when life is not moving fast enough and they feel surrounded by dull, slow-moving people. What happens when your temper explodes? Describe the situation and what you did after the blowout to calm down or resolve the situation.

....
....
....
....
....
....
....
....
....
....
....
....
....
....
....
....
....
....
....
....
....
....

A potentially problematic part of Aries' personality is the inability to complete projects. This is because Mars is an impatient ruler. Take a few minutes to survey your home and notice any projects that have been hanging around for a while unfinished. List them here, then decide which to finish and which to give away or get rid of somehow. Do so without judgment; you are simply clearing up space for projects that interest you.

Aries is a cardinal sign, which means he is a leader—appropriate, since he begins the spring season. Additionally, Aries energy is always battle-ready...sometimes because they provoke conflict; other times because they use their energy to ensure justice and fairness for all. Describe a time when you engaged in battle, metaphorically speaking. What happened? Did you accomplish your mission? How did you feel at the end of the experience?

....

....

....

....

....

....

....

....

....

....

....

....

....

....

....

....

....

....

....

....

....

....

....

....

....

....

....

....

....

....

Music, especially percussion, can be a tonic for Aries. Have you ever thought of playing drums? What kind of music do you like to listen to? Do you like music loud or soft? Describe your relationship to different kinds of music.

Aries can experience muscle cramps and fatigue, since they often prefer quick bursts of speed and short, intense periods of cardio. Be sure to allow your muscles to stretch, relax, and recover after a workout. Have you ever had a deep-tissue massage? What types of massage do you enjoy most? How often do you get a massage? Write about your feelings about massage.

....
....
....
....
....
....
....
....
....
....
....
....
....
....
....
....
....
....
....
....
....
....

Acupuncture is a Mars-ruled therapy because of the use of metal needles to stimulate different meridians of the body. It can address muscle tension and pain as well as protect the body against stress. Have you ever tried acupuncture? Describe any experiences you have had and whether they were helpful. If you haven't tried it, write a list of pros and cons and decide whether to book an appointment.

If you could choose a ruler for the entire world, do you think Aries would be a good choice? Why or why not? Describe your ideal ruler and how they would rule.

Spicy tastes are often favorites of Aries: peppers, garlic, ginger, and so on. What are your favorite dishes to cook or to eat? Describe your reactions to hot sauces. Do you like the spicy burn?

Abundant energy usually brings good health, but Aries is often too busy to focus on their health. Take a moment now to think about your lifestyle choices and write down your typical diet, fitness routine, and sleep habits. Which aspects of these things are you most proud of? Which can you make improvements on?

Aries is usually so eager to get going that they don't think before they act...and sometimes their actions leave a partner or friend out. Do you ever have to work at accommodating or including your mate or partner in your life? Describe a situation when you were sensitive to the other person in a relationship. How did this feel?

....
....
....
....
....
....
....
....
....
....
....
....
....
....
....
....
....
....
....
....
....
....
....
....

As Aries tears through their day, they sometimes are so revved up that falling asleep is difficult. Insomnia provides more time for thoughts and projects—but lack of sleep can be a physical and mental health problem. Describe your sleep habits. What do you do when you can't fall asleep? (Hint: You might want to try moving around and stretching a little to diffuse and calm your energy.)

....
....
....
....
....
....
....
....
....
....
....
....
....
....
....
....
....
....
....
....
....
....

Your symbol, the ram, butts heads with all who cross into their territory. Do you often go head-to-head with people you disagree with? Write about what subjects or personalities can provoke confrontation.

ADDITIONAL RESOURCES

Websites and Other Digital Resources

www.alabe.com

www.astro.com

www.astrodienst.com

www.lunarium.co.uk

www.changingofthegods.com

App: Co-Star

Books

Astrology, Psychology and the Four Elements by Stephen Arroyo

The Astrology of Fate by Liz Greene

Sun Signs by Linda Goodman

Relationship Signs by Linda Goodman

If You Want to Write by Brenda Ueland

The Artist's Way by Julia Cameron

The Hidden Life of Trees by Peter Wohlleben

The Hidden Power of Everyday Things by Constance Stellas, Julie Gillentine, and Jonathan Sharp

Sex Signs by Constance Stellas

The Astrological Guide to Self-Care by Constance Stellas

How to Be an Astrologer by Constance Stellas

The Little Book of Self-Care by Constance Stellas

BIBLIOGRAPHY

Arroyo, Stephen. *Astrology, Psychology and the Four Elements.* Davis, CA: CRCS, 1975.

Arroyo, Stephen. *Relationships & Life Cycles.* Vancouver, WA: CRCS, 1979.

Donath, Emma Belle. *Have We Met Before?* Tempe, AZ: American Federation of Astrologers, 1982.

Forrest, Steven. *The Book of Neptune.* Borrego Springs, CA: Seven Paws, 2016.

Forrest, Steven. *The Book of Fire.* Borrego Springs, CA: Seven Paws, 2019.

Green, Jeffrey Wolf. *Pluto: The Evolutionary Journey of the Soul, Volume I.* St. Paul, MN: Llewellyn, 1985.

Green, Jeffrey Wolf. *Pluto: The Soul's Evolution Through Relationships, Volume II.* St. Paul, MN: Llewellyn, 1997.

Greene, Liz. *The Astrology of Fate.* York Beach, ME: Weiser, 1984.

Hickey, Isabel M. *Astrology: A Cosmic Science.* Sebastopol, CA: CRCS, 2011.

Oken, Alan. *Soul Centered Astrology.* New York: Bantam, 1990.

Sargent, Lois Haines. *How to Handle Your Human Relations.* Tempe, AZ: American Federation of Astrologers, 1958.

Tester, Jim. *A History of Western Astrology.* New York: Ballantine, 1987.

Yott, Donald H. *Astrology and Reincarnation.* York Beach, ME: Weiser, 1989.

DEDICATION

To all those seeking the wisdom in their stars.

ACKNOWLEDGMENTS

I would like to thank Karen Cooper and everyone at Adams Media who helped with this book. To Brendan O'Neill, Katie Corcoran Lytle, Laura Daly, Julia Jacques, Sarah Doughty, Jo-Anne Duhamel, Julia DeGraf, and everyone else who worked on the manuscripts. To Frank Rivera, Priscilla Yuen, Colleen Cunningham, and Tess Armstrong for their work on the book's cover and interior design. I appreciated your team spirit and eagerness to dive into the riches of astrology.

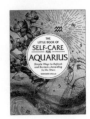